TURKEYS
ON THE FAMILY FARM

Chana Stiefel

Enslow Elementary

an imprint of

 Enslow Publishers, Inc.
40 Industrial Road
Box 398
Berkeley Heights, NJ 07922
USA

http://www.enslow.com

CONTENTS

WORDS TO KNOW

coop—A safe place for turkeys.

flock—A group of turkeys.

hen—A female turkey.

jake—A young male turkey.

poult—A baby turkey.

tom—A male turkey.

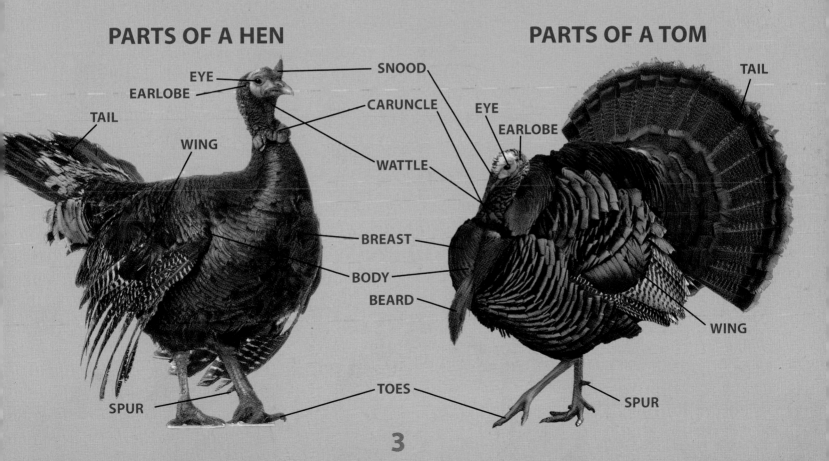

PARTS OF A HEN

PARTS OF A TOM

EYE

EARLOBE

TAIL

WING

SNOOD

CARUNCLE

WATTLE

EYE

EARLOBE

TAIL

BREAST

BODY

BEARD

WING

SPUR

TOES

SPUR

3

EYE SPY

Did you know that
a turkey can see
100 yards away?
That's the length
of a football field!
Find out more
fun facts about turkeys
on the family farm.

GOBBLE,
GOBBLE

Tara, Matt, Jack and young Alice
are ready for the day.

Up to 100 turkeys live on Matt and Tara's farm. The family raises many other animals, too. Their children, Jack and Alice, help with the chores.

tom

jake

poult

hen

Name game: A male turkey is called a tom or "gobbler."
A female is a hen. Baby turkeys are called poults.
Young male turkeys are jakes. A group of turkeys is a flock.

The farmers check on the turkeys every day. If one gets sick, Matt will take it away from the flock. He may change its food. He may give it a healing plant to eat.

TURKEY
FEED

During the day, the **flock** runs around outside. They eat grass and plants. Turkeys' feet have sharp nails for digging. They dig up acorns, nuts, and seeds. Turkeys even find worms and bugs to eat! They drink water.

A turkey's sharp nails help it dig up food.

COOP
GROUP

Young turkeys live inside a fence. It protects them from hungry animals, like foxes.

At night, the turkeys nest inside a **coop**. The coop looks like a big tent. It rests on wheels. Jack helps roll the coop down the field each day. This way, the turkeys always have fresh grass to eat.

The farmers roll the coop to a new spot every day.

snood

caruncle

wattle

FUNNY
FACES

A **tom** turkey looks different from a **hen**. A tom's head has more lumpy parts. When a tom gets excited, these parts fill with blood. They turn red.

FEATHERED
FRIENDS

A tom's feathers are more colorful than a hen's feathers. Its tail feathers spread open. They look like a fan. The fan makes the tom look bigger and stronger. Toms shake their feathers to make hens notice them.

Toms strut around and display their fans so hens will spot them.

BABY
TURKEYS

Baby turkeys are **poults**. They are bigger than baby chicks. Their necks are longer, too. Poults eat grass and bugs. Matt and Tara also feed them grain, dried fish meal, seaweed, and hard-boiled eggs. Alice helps feed the baby turkeys.

Poults are kept warm in the barn. The farmers move the turkeys to the coop when they are seven or eight weeks old.

Matt, Tara, and Alice sell the vegetables they grow, too.

18

HOLIDAY
TURKEYS

The turkeys are raised for meat. People come to the farm to buy fresh turkey for their holiday dinners. The turkeys may weigh 8 to 25 pounds.

Matt and Tara's biggest holiday turkey weighed 34 pounds.

DIFFERENT TYPES OF TURKEYS

Not all turkeys are the same. Turkeys have many breeds. See how different they look? Which one is your favorite?

Naragansett

Bourbon Red

White Holland

LIFE CYCLE OF A TURKEY

1. A turkey hen lays 10 to 14 eggs in her nest. Turkey eggs are about twice the size of chicken eggs. After about 28 days, the eggs hatch.

2. Poults are bigger than chicks. They have long necks. By eight weeks, their feathers have grown in.

3. One-year-old turkeys are adults. Turkeys may live eight to ten years.

LEARN MORE

BOOKS

Endres, Holly. *Turkeys*. Minneapolis, Minn.: Bellwether Media, 2008.

Falwell, Cathryn. *Gobble, Gobble*. Nevada City, Calif.:
Dawn Publications, 2011.

Marsico, Katie. *Turkeys*. Ann Arbor, Mich.: Cherry Lake Pub., 2011.

WEB SITES

California Foundation for Agriculture in the Classroom.
<http://www.learnaboutag.org/turkeytour/activityguide.pdf>

Kids Farm.
<http://www.kidsfarm.com/farm.htm>

INDEX

Enslow Elementary, an imprint of Enslow Publishers, Inc.
Enslow Elementary® is a registered trademark of Enslow Publishers, Inc.

Copyright © 2013 by Chana Stiefel

Library of Congress Cataloging-in-Publication Data
Stiefel, Chana, 1968-
Turkeys on the family farm / Chana Stiefel.
p. cm. — (Animals on the family farm)
Summary: "An introduction to an animal's life on a farm for early readers. Find out what a turkey eats, where it lives, and what they are like on a farm"—Provided by publisher.
Includes index.
ISBN 978-0-7660-4207-0
1. Turkeys—Juvenile literature. I. Title. II. Series: Animals on the family farm.
SF507.S74 2014
636.5'92—dc23
2012028806

Future editions:
Paperback ISBN: 978-1-4644-0357-6
Single-User ISBN: 978-1-4646-1197-1
EPUB ISBN: 978-1-4645-1197-4
Multi-User ISBN: 978-0-7660-5829-3

Printed in China
012013 Leo Paper Group, Heshan City, Guangdong, China
10 9 8 7 6 5 4 3 2 1

To Our Readers: We have done our best to make sure all Internet Addresses in this book were active and appropriate when we went to press. However, the author and the publisher have no control over and assume no liability for the material available on those Internet sites or on other Web sites they may link to. Any comments or suggestions can be sent by e-mail to comments@enslow.com or to the address on the back cover.

Photo Credits: AP Images/The Shelbyville News, Carol Swartz, p. 20–21; Photos.com: fdevalera, p. 9, Sarah Kennedy, p. 10; Gould Academy/Tracey Wilkerson, p. 11; Howling Wolf Farm, pp. 6, 8, 18; © iStockphoto.com/Rehlik, p. 22 (poults); Roger Tidman/FLPA/Minden Pictures, p. 15; Shutterstock.com, pp. 1, 2, 3, 4–5, 7 (tom, jake, poult), 12, 13, 14, 16, 17, 19, 20, 21, 22 (eggs, adult); © WILDLIFE GmbH/Alamy, p. 7 (hen).

Cover Photo: Shutterstock.com

A note from Matt and Tara of Howling Wolf Farm: Howling Wolf Farm grows vital food to feed individuals and families. Products include vegetables, dry beans and grains, dairy, beef, eggs, chicken, lamb, and pork. We work in partnership with nature and people to grow vibrant, abundant food. We farm with an intention of creating a farm and food to bring health, vitality, and enjoyment to our complete beings and the land. We focus on heirloom and open-pollinated varieties, heritage breeds, and wild foods.

Series Science Consultant:
Dana Palmer
Sr. Extension Associate/4-H Youth Outreach
Department of Animal Science
Cornell University
Ithaca, NY

Series Literacy Consultant:
Allan A. De Fina, Ph.D.
Past President of the New Jersey
Reading Association
Dean of the College of Education
New Jersey City University
Jersey City, NJ